A Practical Professional Development Framework Guide
for First Nation Leaders, Government Leaders, and
Not-for-Profit Government Organizations who interact
with Canadian Indigenous People

Strengthening
Canadian Indigenous

Relationships And Decision-Making Processes

Dr. Cathy A. Martin, Ed.D.
Listuguj Mi'gmaq First Nation

Tellwell Talent

www.tellwell.ca

ISBN

9780-2-2881-352-1 (Paperback)

Table of Contents

Acknowledgements

I would like to thank my editor and *Nidabèskw* Jessica L. Metallic, M.Ed. for her editorial skills and personal encouragement with this endeavour. *Wela'lin.*

Introduction

This professional development tool was designed as a facilitation solution to help First Nations community leaders maintain their traditional values, while making decisions that reflect the direction of their people. These decisions must then be conveyed in a manner understandable by the Federal, Provincial, and Territorial (FPT) Governments, whom First Nation leaders often contend with for communal governance and prosperity. Often FPT government leaders are unfamiliar with the underlying cultural values that influence the direction of First Nation politicians. In contrast, First Nation leaders often have difficulty relating to the underlying cultural values inferred in the hierarchical structures used in communication and decision-making by other governments.

This framework tool is further refined to incorporate not-for-profit, non-government organizations (NGOs) that provide services and policies for Indigenous grassroots people, in order that these groups have a better understanding of each other; thereby, strengthening working relationships. Often NGOs are staffed by non-Indigenous people, or passionate urban-Indigenous people, who have the best of intentions, but may lack the direct experience, the cultural values, and knowledge of the community realities and needs of our Indigenous peoples.

The motivation for creating these working frameworks stems from my experiences and opinions as a political leader within a First Nation community and the experiences of working in various urban non-for-profit governmental organizations (NGOs) as a grass-roots First Nation community member. The theories used in the underlying values system stem from academic research. The practical frameworks illustrated, were developed based on identification of a need for tool(s) to help these groups better facilitate communication and decision-making with each other and among themselves.

The Origins of Structures

Holistic versus Hierarchical

When we examine the organizational structures imbedded in our cultures, we must first trace these cultural practices to basic human needs and survival. For simplicity, a contrast exists between cultures that thrive on either a holistic approach for basic needs and survival, or a hierarchical approach. Both these approaches can be theorized as evolving from our basic human need for acceptance. Humans are social animals that need others to feel safe or provide protection from danger. Basic human contact is also necessary. The acceptance of others can first be determined in the common values of a given culture.

Holistic Cultures

In holistic cultures, acceptance is obtained by the practice of unconditional inclusion, which is based on internal values of trust, honesty, love, respect and humility. In these cultures, survival is achieved by the practice of working as an extended family wherein everyone has each other's back. As a people, every person has specific roles and responsibilities within the family/tribe to ensure the group can exist. If any member of the group does not uphold their responsibility, the whole group suffers; subsequently, resolve is sought by input from the whole group. In discussions involving the sustainability of the group, every voice is heard and respected – everyone is viewed as equal: man, woman, and child.

A cultural example of this could be described in a tribal village setting as follows: Hunters are needed to go and hunt the game. Elders or knowledge holders are needed to guide the process of safe food preparation. Food preparers, cooks, servers, cleaners, etc. are all needed. Trust and accountability are needed to ensure efficiency. Leaders emerge to ensure everyone eats. Leaders ensure that food is distributed according to need rather than equality. All people are loved and valued for their contribution to the feast, without status or judgement. Great hunters are humbled by the talents of the artists who can create works of art from the remnants of the animals; and the children are humbled by the teachings of the knowledge holders. Hence, everyone eats based on unconditional inclusion and contribution, for the survival of the whole. Many Indigenous communities, globally, still implement the core values of this holistic approach to sustainability in their way of life.

Hierarchical Cultures

In hierarchical cultures, acceptance is obtained by merit through the practices of recognition and categorization. The values in hierarchical cultures are external, including awards, status, power, time, and money. In these cultures, survival is dependant upon personal achievement by the perception of others. Beginning with the underlying assumption that you must constantly improve your skills, be in competition with others, and to obtain a higher rank in the category you have chosen. Strategies for personal gain require a level of secrecy, with limited confidence that others will help you, especially if they are trying to gain something similar. You remain accountable for your actions, and if necessary, others determine your consequences. Leaders in hierarchical structures, usually, have earned their status by climbing the ranks in their classification. Discussions for resolutions or planning are usually conducted with those of similar rank in one's given category or classification; in some cases, without the input of those who are impacted by the decisions. People in hierarchical cultures have learned to always be on guard as acceptance is conditional and you remain in competition to the group for whom you wish to belong.

An example of a hierarchical culture is a society that is evolved around business and commerce. Chains of command are in order, as plans and communication are structured and regulated. Skills must be proven even before you are considered to compete to be part of a given business. Time is a conditional factor, as deadlines are necessary to evaluate and continue progress. Profits or production are the ultimate goal. Competition and strategic planning are needed to achieve more than another business with similar commerce. When leaders of the same company make decisions, they speak with those who share a common vision, and have common interests and skill sets. For example, an automobile manufacturer is not likely to seek the opinion of a carpenter. Input is mainly received from experts in the automotive industry; yet, most carpenters drive vehicles. Bonuses and awards are distributed to those who have earned them, not for those who are in need of recognition or appreciation. Many government organizations, and not-for-profit government organizations have adopted this culture.

Holistic Culture Value Practices within a Bureaucracy

Trust – Based on the understanding that each individual is part of team and is needed to ensure results; trust that quality work will be produced after general direction has been agreed upon. This eliminates the need for micro-management, as initial trust has been established upon the competencies proven within the hiring process and probationary period.

Honesty - Honesty is best exhibited by accountability. Taking responsibility for the work you have committed to doing is based on this value. If there exists any foreseen or emergent reason that prevent you from to completing the task at hand, strategizing with the team on how to overcome this barrier is done as quickly as possible. Being able to present obstacles requires you to be honest about your developing skills and trust in the collaboration of the team, rather than receiving harsh judgement from others. There exist no excuses for not completing the task, but rather, remaining accountable to being part of a larger process that is solution-oriented.

Love – Love in the bureaucratic setting is best displayed by the acceptance of others' unique personalities and perspectives as part of the team. Acceptance of the differences displayed by others avoids the toxicity of gossip in the workplace; rather, love creates a safe workplace where employees can be themselves, and appreciate the value that each person brings to the team. As humans, we tend to relate better to those who think, look, and act similar to us. However, the value of unconditional acceptance allows us to analyze the traits of those who annoy us, and determine the value their uniqueness brings to the team. For example: A co-worker's bluntness may be annoying, but you love the way they can negotiate a bargain.

Respect – Respect in a bureaucratic setting does not solely exist amongst co-workers or within the confines of the organization. Respect is the consideration given to how your work or decisions affect other organizations, the target population of your work, the general population, and the effect your work has on future generations. Good communication is essential in respectful relationships. Agreement is not always possible within any professional relationship, but acknowledgement of others' point-of-view is always possible.

Humility – Humility is based on the belief we are all life-long learners. In bureaucratic organizations, we have a shared vision guiding us to achieve a particular goal. How we obtain that vision can be derived from an infinite number of possibilities. The value of humility is practiced when we can open our minds to the various perspectives of others, who bring to the table a diverse set of skills and experiences. As social beings, we continually learn from the experiences of others. Supremacy based on age or experience hinders the ingenuity of accepting and considering the valued input of all team players with equal acknowledgement.

Hierarchical Culture Values practices within a Bureaucracy

Time – Time is a common measure in which we all share equally, but how each of us choose to use that time varies. Time is placed on the bottom rung of the bureaucratic later. Being able to achieve a goal sooner than others puts you a step above the rest into proving your acceptance into the group. Time is a competitive element in the race to the top; thus, time constraints produce an element of internal stress. On another note, timelines and deadlines are useful for ensuring tasks are completed and ready for use, either to realize the next level of an overall task, or to be effectively communicated with others for continued progress or negotiation.

Awards – Awards are given to someone who has met a criterion set by a group to acknowledge the merit of an individual(s), who seeks to belong to and progress within the category chosen by the group. In bureaucracy, the first award is acceptance into the group as a selected employee who competed and "won" the job by proving to have best meet the criteria as such. Awards can continue to occur in the form of bonuses, promotions, seniority privileges, and other benefits usually based on an employee's performance in comparison to other employees in the organization. Awards can be an incentive for motivation for employees to achieve greater acceptance within the organization. Awards can also help employees climb the organizational ladder to higher recognition and status. The competitiveness of awards can result in employees working in "silos" with personal agendas, rather than truly working together to achieve a common goal. While awards glorify one, the lack of awards for those who contribute to the best of their ability has a detrimental affect on the said individual, and in-turn the organization.

Money - The value of money is said to be one of the most motivational factors in a hierarchical structure. Money is so attractive because it gives the perception of success. Money can buy possessions and hierarchical status, which in turn can be viewed as powerful. Money can influence acceptance into chosen groups, not just groups that are aligned with your skills and interest, but any group that shares the perception that money equates success. The value of money, and the ability to obtain more by individuals, or for the organization, even those not-for-profit, can disregard anything and everything that does not promote increased monetary value; including underlying organizational goals, policies, and overall acts of compassion for humanity. However, without money to pay individuals and expenses, most organizations could not exist, prosper, or manage effectively. Money is a necessity in today's society, but if overvalued as an indicator for success and acceptance, it can cause a spiral of immorality.

Status – Status is a recognition of prestige, respect, and esteem that is given to an individual by the judgement of others. In organizations of hierarchical culture, status is sought by individuals through merit and networking. Employees seeking higher ranks on the organizational ladder typically display kindness and cooperativeness to co-workers in an attempt to be viewed worthy of promotions or positions of social status. It can be argued that the quest for higher status is a motivator for employees to work harder to realize the vision of the organization. However, the value of obtaining increased status has the primary objective of self-serving personal gain through the aforementioned vision of the organization.

Power – Power in the bureaucratic setting is the position of control over critical resources, including human and monetary resources. Those who value power, often begin by establishing higher status; yet many employees in higher-status positions do not value power and are content with upper levels of input without the power. The key difference is people who prefer high status over power, value people and relationships that contributed to their attainment of status, while people of power tend to be dismissive and are primarily viewed as those with the ability to obtain resources and manage them effectively. Obtaining funding is a necessity for organizations to function and prosper. However, persons of power are viewed as disconnected to the employees in the lower ranks, thereby creating division or categories within the same organization.

Summary of Holistic and Hierarchical Practices

Holistic	Hierarchical
Based on internal values such as love, trust, honesty, respect, and humility	Based on external values such as awards, status, power, and money
Inclusive- everyone is respected equally, despite type of social contribution	Exclusive – Respect is earned in selected categories
Openness of discussion for the greater good	Secrecy of strategy for self-gain
Sense of Safety - Trust that others have your back as you have theirs	Constant stress and suspicion - Watch your back, it' every person for themselves.
Lack of accountability results in negative consequences for all	Lack of accountability hurts mainly self
Restorative measures are used to rectify situations	Punitive measures to rectify situations
Trust that matters will be realized in due time, when the timing is right, and that matters have a way of resolving themselves.	Time is critical, planning is linear, deadlines determine efficiency of goals
Focus on relationships of amongst humans	Focus on achievement, results, and profit
Everyone is taken care of based on need, rather than level of effort	Level of effort/achievement determines amount of award
Decisions affecting the group are strategized from the perspective of all, regardless of age, capabilities, and skills	Decisions affecting the group are strategized from similar perspectives, according to proven skills and capabilities
Consensus is sought	Majority prevails

Merging of Holistic and Hierarchical Practices for Better Communication

When we analyze the difference between value systems from the holistic way of life and the hierarchical way of conduct, we begin to see how stress and discontent manifests within and amongst organizations with similar visions. Confusion and frustration begin to emerge within leaders of the organizations as their underlying values do not match the underlying values of the leaders from partner organizations, who are in working together for a common goal.

First Nation leaders, at the grassroots level, such as elected Chief and Councils, Hereditary Chief and Councils, and First Nation directors living within their communities, often struggle with their underlying holistic values while trying to prosper in a hierarchical society. Not only do they struggle with working in hierarchal systems, they struggle to maintain their underlying, inherited values while making decisions to govern in comparison to their surrounding governments. Thus, their holistic values based on trust for the betterment of the tribe and respect of equality is compromised when making decisions at the community level.

Similarly, leaders in federal, provincial, and territorial governments, and directors of organizations created for the general benefit of Indigenous people, often struggle to understand the work patterns of conduct within First Nation communities, while trying to meet the requirements of the hierarchical structures within their organization's policies. Often in their attempts to portray inclusiveness of the First Nation population they work with or advocate for, these organizations seek to hire people of Indigenous descent.

However, positions are seldom filled by grassroots First Nation people who have lived in their communities within the past five years, for a number of reasons. In hierarchical structures, perceptions of others are valued, so people of Indigenous descent are thus needed, resulting in the hiring of what some people view as the "token First Nation." This person can be described as an Indigenous employee who is hired to give perspective and input on behalf of the Indigenous peoples of the entire country! There are both pros and cons to this, and much discussion on this controversial approach for First Nation input can be debated.

With such a contrast between the two systems of conduct within organizations, is it possible to merge the two to create a framework to have the best of both worlds? The answer is yes, absolutely. There are elements of value in both systems of governance. To establish a workable framework incorporating the two systems, we can focus on the inclusiveness and trust from the holistic values and the timeliness and results of the hierarchical values.

Some First Nation governments, other governments, and various organizations serving Indigenous populations have developed their own frameworks to help guide their facilitation of decision-making processes, to improve communications and build relationships between and within organizations in relation to Indigenous people. The following two templates can be used or adapted to create the best practice for decision-making that incorporates key elements from both the holistic and hierarchical structures:

1. First Nations Social Based Governance Model
2. Intergovernmental Policy Developing Model for Respecting First Nations

First Nations Social Based Governance Model

The following First Nations Social Based Governance Model is a community-driven, decision-making tool developed with the objective of respecting the cultural inclusiveness of decision making. This tool is to be used as a guide to help Chiefs and Councils serve their communities in a way that best represents their Nation's direction. This tool can address any issue and works well in communities that practice portfolio holding councillors. This tool can be adapted to fit the unique needs of any given Indigenous community.

The first step for using this tool, is to identify an issue. Once an issue has been identified, the following information is to sought in order to best understand the issue from various perspectives and with respect to various considerations. Following a gathering of information, a plan of action template is recommended.

This information is collected, ideally under the direction of the portfolio holder or designated staff. The information is then presented to Chief and Council at a duly convened meeting for discussion and decision-making, using the following Action Plan format: Once Actions have been aligned with person(s) responsible and a deadline has been set, then the adoption of the Action Plan is set for motion by council.

FIRST NATIONS SOCIAL-BASED GOVERNANCE MODEL ©
Community Driven Decision-Making Tool

Issue: _____   ISSUE # _____

Pertinent Directorates/Departments: _____

Date identified, start of process: _____

Director's and Executive Staff Comments (measures already in place/policies)	General Department Staff comments	Community Members Comments	Tribal councils Comments	Elders' Comments	Future Generation Implications/ Nation Responsibilities	Off reserve membership Considerations	Legal Obligations (human rights, Canadian Labour Board)	Financial Implications	Other Considerations

CHIEF AND COUNCIL PLAN OF ACTION ©

ISSUE: _____ ISSUE # _____

DATE OF ACTION PLAN: _____

Motioned by: _____ Seconded by: _____

Abstentions: _____ Opposed: _____ Absent: _____

Action Items	Person(s) responsible *Must name actual person(s) not department	Implementation Deadline	Timeline for Feedback	Follow-Up Report Dates 1. Chief and Council 2. Community	Date completed

Intergovernmental Policy Developing Model for Respecting Indigenous Populations

Federal, Provincial, and Territorial Governments (FPTs), as well as National Indigenous Organizations (NIOs), and not-for-profit government organizations (NGOs), who provide services for Indigenous people, develop policies that affect the governance, service delivery, and interaction amongst the Indigenous populations within Canada. Policies are developed to have a pre-established guideline that can assist in the best management of any given issue. Some of the key elements in establishing any policy include:

- Defining the necessity of the policy
- Establishing a process to create the policy within a realistic timeline
- Research of what is current common practice pertaining to the given issue; and identifying efforts that have already been tried in addressing the given issue or situation
- Meaningful consultation with the group your policy is intended for
- Presenting draft policy, which was developed based on meaningful consultation, to both the decision-makers and the group the policy was created for
- Receive feedback and discussion, then revise draft policy
- Present revised policy for review, then adoption by the decision-makers
- Note any major disagreements of content within if necessary
- Once policy is adopted, set timelines for review and revision of the developed policy in order that the policy stays relevant with the times and issue at hand

This common pattern for policy development may have variations, but the key element in any policy for compliance and acceptance is including meaningful input from the population you are writing the policy for. If the population is not adequately consulted; if the policy objective fails to adequately define the problem; or if the policy makers have biased opinions, then the policy is considered defective. Poorly developed policies result in discontent, dissatisfaction, and/or non-compliance of the said group; thus, rendering the policy ineffective in resolving or managing the intended issue.

Another major obstacle in developing effective policies is the possibility of change in policy-makers or changes in decision-makers or key informants representing the said population. In both FPT governments and individual communities' Chief and Council governments, the possibility of change among key players is often at risk due to elections or high turn-over rates of government employees. High turn-over rates are also not uncommon in not-for-profit government organizations who serve Indigenous populations.

In respectful recognition of the work in policy development by Federal, Provincial and Territorial governments and not-for-profit government organizations that have years of experience in policy development; the following oversights have been observed and thus, are noted in relation to developing policies in the best interest of Indigenous populations:

- Blanket approaches do not adequately represent the diversity among Indigenous peoples. First Nations, Inuit, and Metis are very distinct in cultures and rights. Furthermore, even among the given Indigenous Nations diversity exists. The biggest assumption that FPT governments and NGOs make is that all First Nations are the same or very similar. While this may be true to a certain extent, each First Nation community remains distinct in their own way of life, beliefs, and culture, and are governed by their own elected and/or hereditary leaders; as such, they are considered as their own Nation and should be treated as such.
- Establishing timelines for policy development should include adequate time for mean-ingful consultation with the people living within the communities affected by the policy. Their policy review and feedback, and most importantly their acceptance of the final policy for their community need to also be allotted within the established timeline. Often FPT governments and NGOs consume an ample amount of time preparing for

and drafting policies; yet, often when presented to, often sporadic, representation of the Indigenous population, strict and unreasonable timeframes to gather meaningful input are unilaterally imposed.

- The communication approach for gathering input from the population that the developing policy is intended to represent should include representation from **each** Indigenous community represented. At first glance, this may seem like an overwhelming task, as there are hundreds of distinct Inuit, Metis, and First Nations communities within Canada. However, the suggested *"Policy Development Framework for Improving Inclusiveness of Indigenous Input"* below can be used or adapted to better facilitate representative input from the distinct communities. Many appreciated efforts by FPT governments and NGOs to include Indigenous input have been exercised by employing an Indigenous person on staff or for policy development project; however, one or few individuals cannot possibly give the perspective and background from the whole of each grassroots or urban Indigenous community. Their input is helpful, perhaps, depending on their experiences, to offer an overall perspective or offer a description to help non-Indigenous better understand the lifestyles common to most Indigenous communities; but their input should not constitute as a substitute for meaningful consultation, review, and acceptance of policy. Another caution to consider as a substitute for meaningful community input is the use of regional or national Indigenous offices. Although these organizations can be useful in helping to gather direct input from the various communities, their sole input should not be constituted as a substitute for meaningful consultation, review, or acceptance of policy, unless they have been legally delegated to do so via way of resolution by the individual communities.

Hence, the suggested use of the following framework can help create meaningful policies that are based on general common issues; yet, respectful of community inclusion and allowance for community uniqueness, and community-driven decision making during the adoption stage of the given policy. Needless to say, copies of the policy must then be distributed to the applicable population.

Policy Developing Framework for Improving Inclusion of Indigenous Nations Input ©

Policy Objective: (describe briefly)

Policy Commonalities: (attach an initial draft of proposed options for the policy development of a given issue)

Name of Community:

Nationality: (Tribe of First Nation, Inuit, or Metis)

Population of Community:

On reserve: _____ **Urban/off reserve:** _____

Identification of Contact person for community, as appointed by recognized leadership, i.e.: resolution or letter: _____ (This person may be a band-member, or elected member of council, portfolio holder, director, or key administrator, etc. as delegated)

Contact information for Contact person: (include email, telephone, mailing address, and direct supervisor or alternate contact). The person identified for contact remains responsible for ensuring communication and consultation of the proposed policy occurs within the community. This may be done in collaboration with regional or external agencies or other staff members, but the responsibility and liaison relationship with FPT government and NGO representatives remains with the contact person.

Establishment of mutual deadlines with Community Contact:

- **Deadline for introduction of policy/identified issue:**
- **Deadline for initial consult of all groups:**
- **Deadline for report of input from community (all relevant groups from chart below) to FPT or NGO representative:**
- **Deadline for collaborative policy development:**
- **Deadline for community review:**
- **Deadline for collaborative revision and notation of major differences or situations that impacted the process (ex: turn-over, disagreements among opinions within community):**
- **Deadline for adaptation by leadership:**
- **Establishment of period policy review:**

Community input venue: (identify all sources of information gathering, including but not limited to: surveys (in person, online), working groups, public meetings, etc..)

Consideration of the following groups consulted:

Group	Venue	Number of participants
Elected leaders		
Hereditary Leaders		
Urban members		
Community members		
Elders		
Youth		
Impact on environment		
Impact on surrounding communities/relations		
Other considerations		

Identification of any pre-existing bi-laws or oral laws of understanding relating to the identified issue of policy at hand:

MONTSERRAT, Our Home

Life with a Lava Dome

Written & Illustrated by Sonja Melander

Printed by CreateSpace, an Amazon.com company

Montserrat, Emerald Isle, in the Caribbean Sea,
With birds and mangoes and lush green trees.

In the sparkling water all around,
A rainbow of fish and coral can be found.

Beneath the ground, way down below,
Are magma and gas, feeding the volcano.

This is our volcano, the Soufrière Hills.
Come, let's explore how it builds and builds!

Since 1995 when the latest eruption began,
Montserrat's shore has grown out in a fan.

When lava in the dome piles up high,
Our island grows higher into the sky.

up... and up...

Our neighborhood volcano isn't new.
From seafloor to sky it slowly grew.

and UP!▶

Millions of years have passed since the time,
That the magma began its upward climb.

Soufrière Hills Volcano
Active NOW

South Soufrière Hills
Active 130 Thousand years ago

Volcanic eruptions throughout history,
Built these green hills poking out from the sea.

Centre Hills
Active 950 to 550 Thousand years ago

Silver Hills
Active 2.6 to 1.2 Million years ago

In the valleys around our volcano lie,
Ash-covered buildings that are empty and dry...

Plymouth, before 1995

Bramble Airport and Plymouth, our capital city,
Now are lost, when once lively and pretty.

Pyroclastic flows are hot winds of stone and ash,
Which can move faster than an Olympic dash.

Rushing down valleys, they follow each bend,
But they can sweep over hills and swiftly descend.

They burn or smash all they travel upon,
And can bury buildings until they're gone.

In an instant they make charcoal from trees.
Never ever get in the way of one of these!

When this flow quickly enters the sea,
It can make a deadly tsunami.

Tsunamis form when water is shoved away.
Out to sea they're small, but they grow taller in the bay!

Lahars are mudflows made of water and ash.
They carry huge boulders that mash and crash.

They form when rushing water drains,
Over volcanic ash during heavy rains.

As a lahar gathers debris it can quickly grow,
from a gentle trickle...

To a scary mudflow!

Volcanic ash isn't like the ash from burnt wood.
It's itchy and sharp and just not very good.

volcanic ash

KABOOM!

SMASH!

It's made when lava explodes or rock is smashed to bits.
It falls from ash clouds to the ground where it sits...

It can harm buildings, so we sweep it off.
We wear ash masks because it makes us cough.

Ash lofts in the air, making it hard to see.
As it floats on the wind, there's nowhere to flee.

When ash is carried on the breeze,
It can endanger other places across the seas.

Ash in the sky can travel many miles.
Our volcano's ash has gone to neighboring isles.

Eastern Caribbean Islands
and their volcanoes

Saba
Mt. Scenery

Statia
The Quill

St. Kitts
Mt. Liamuiga

Nevis
Nevis Peak

Montserrat
Soufrière Hills

Guadeloupe
La Soufrière

Dominica
Morne Aux Diables
Morne Diablotins
Morne Trois Piton
Wotten Waven/Micotrin
Morne Watt
Valley of Desolation
Morne Anglais
Grand Soufrière Hills
Plat Plays Volcanic Complex

Martinique
Mt. Pelée

St. Vincent
La Soufrière

St. Lucia
Soufrière Volcanic Centre

Grenada ← Kick 'Em Jenny
underwater volcano

N
W   E
S

Other places near Montserrat have volcanoes too.
One of them is still underwater and new.

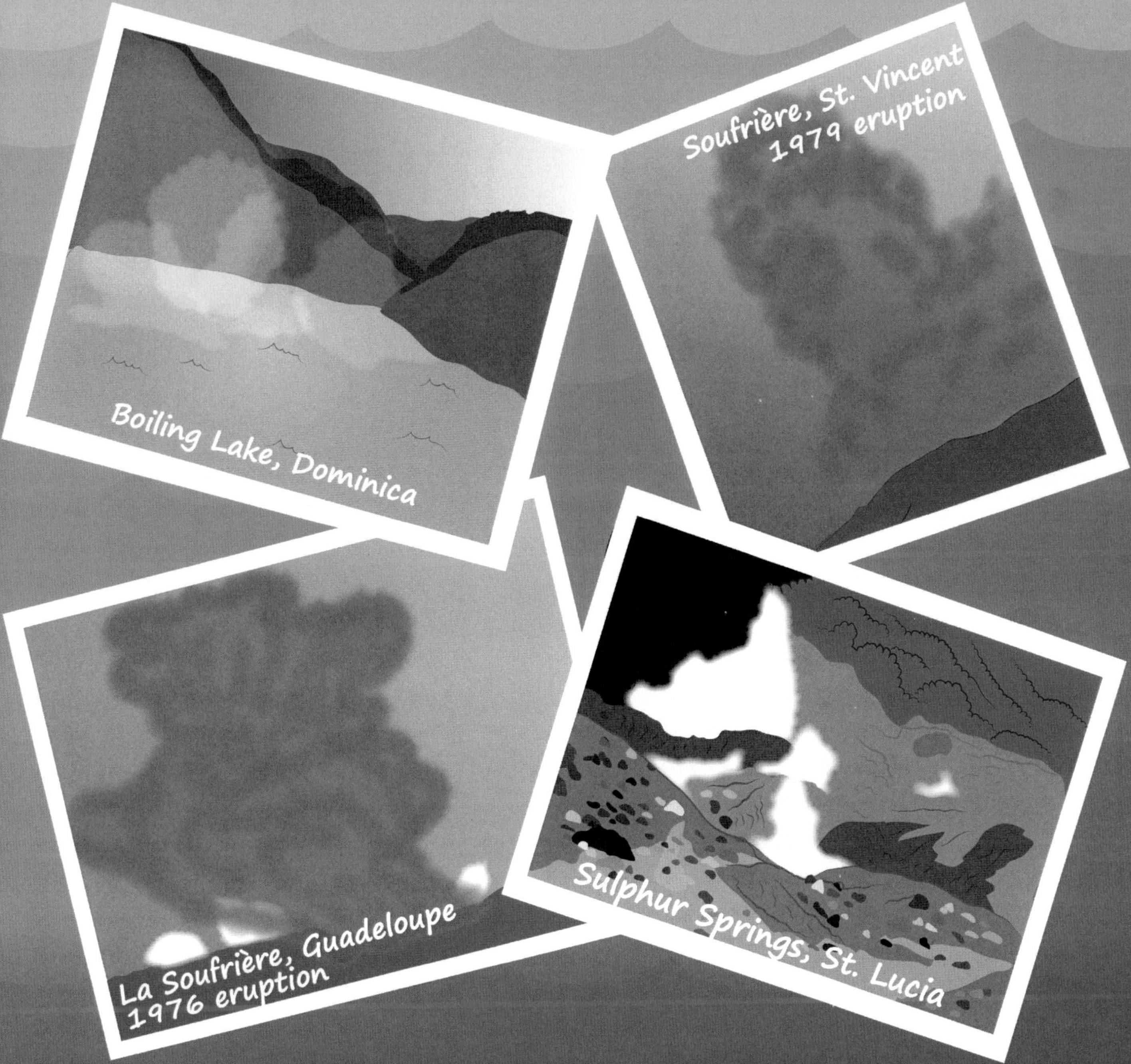

Boiling Lake, Dominica

Soufrière, St. Vincent
1979 eruption

La Soufrière, Guadeloupe
1976 eruption

Sulphur Springs, St. Lucia

Most aren't active now, but they could wake up one day,
And cause a disaster like at Mt. Pelèe...

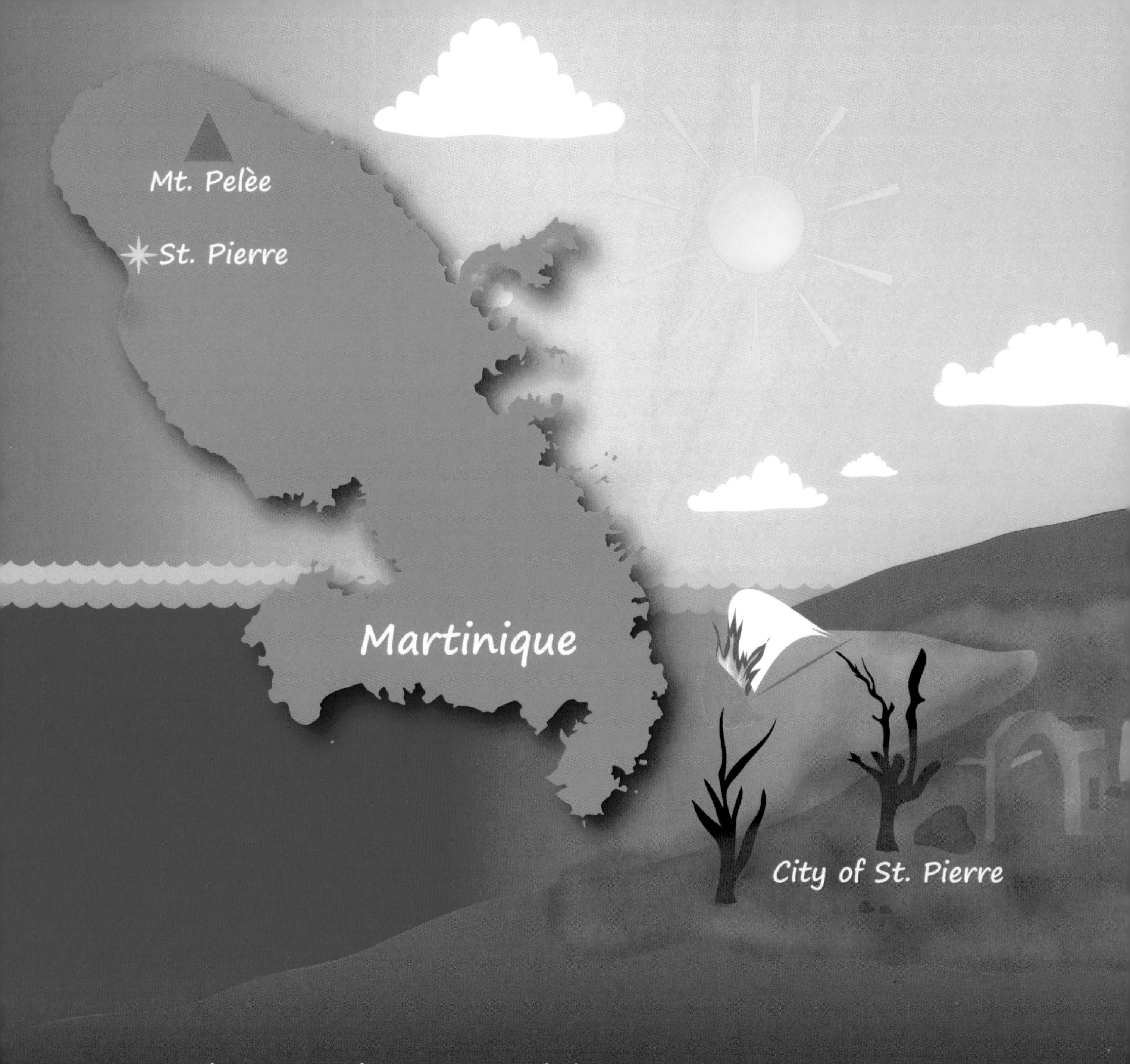

Mt. Pelèe

St. Pierre

Martinique

City of St. Pierre

That eruption on Martinique over a century ago,
Killed 29,000 people in a pyroclastic flow.

Mt. Pelèe Volcano

So such a tragedy does not happen another time,
Scientists watch volcanoes for any warning sign...

These scientists are volcanologists. What do they do?
They watch the volcano to see what it's up to!

Volcanoes are monitored in several ways,
To see if they're active or in a paused phase

Scientists can measure gas that tells,
If inside the volcano new magma dwells.

Sulfur, carbon dioxide, and steam,
Can leave the volcano with a roar and a scream.

new digital seismometer

old seismometer

STATION 1

They also use seismometers to sense,
Magma moving toward volcanic vents.

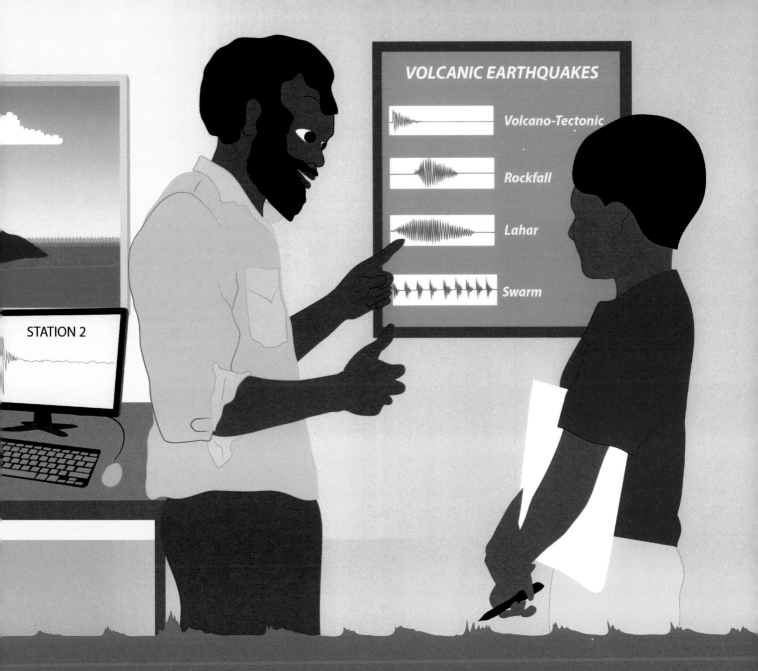

Volcanic flows can also make an earthquake,
When boulders collide with the ground and shake.

magma rises and
builds pressure

Magma can slowly change the shape of the land.
As magma gathers below, the surface above can expand.

GPS satellites

GPS receiver

This is measured by special equipment which tells,
Just how much the ground shrinks or swells.

Special thermal cameras can see a warm spot.
If our eyes see it glowing, we know it's REALLY hot!

These tools help volcanologists to keep watch and see,
In case something happens suddenly!

For now it's forbidden to enter the space,
Near the volcano, just in case...
There is a sudden flow or blast...
Think you can run to escape? NOBODY is that fast!

This place is called the exclusion zone.
Inside is a world buried beneath ash and stone.

Soufrière Hills Volcano on the Emerald Isle,
   May continue to brew for awhile.
      Our little island may see more disruption,
         Like a lahar, ashfall, or a new eruption.

Even with dangers from the lava dome,
Montserrat is still our beloved home.
Our dear island still glistens with life and charm,
Just stay to the north, away from harm.

Glossary

ash- Tiny pieces of rock made by a volcano. Ash ranges in size from about the size of powdered sugar to the size of a pencil tip.

carbon dioxide- (CO_2) A gas released by volcanoes made of carbon and oxygen.

deformation- Changes in the ground shape around an active volcano, which are usually (but not always) very small. The land around an active volcano can swell up (inflation) when magma is building pressure underground. After a volcanic eruption, the land often shrinks back (deflates) due to the release of pressure.

DOAS- (Differential Optical Absorption Spectroscopy) A technique used by scientists to measure the amount of different kinds of gases, like sulfur dioxide, coming out of a volcano. Scientists are able to measure the gases by measuring sunlight through a cloud of gas and comparing it to sunlight that didn't go through the cloud of gas.

dome- See "lava dome"

exclusion zone- The area around the volcano that people are not allowed to go into. It is extremely dangerous to be in this zone (even when the volcano seems quiet) because lava domes can collapse without warning, creating dangerous pyroclastic flows.

fan- The fan-shaped deposit of ash and rock deposited by a pyroclastic flow. In 2010, a single pyroclastic flow deposited so much ash and rock in a fan that the shoreline moved out to sea over 500 meters from where it was before!

GPS- (Global Positioning System) A system that uses satellites to measure the exact location of a GPS receiver on the ground. By measuring the exact location of GPS receivers (to within a few millimeters) over and over, volcanologists can measure deformation of the area around a volcano.

hazard map- A map that shows what areas might be affected in the future by volcanic hazards, like pyroclastic flows, lahars, and ashfall. Hazard maps are made by volcanologists in a few ways, usually by figuring out what areas have been affected by volcanic hazards in the past and by using computer simulations that model what might happen in future volcanic eruptions.

hydrogen sulfide- (H_2S) A gas released by volcanoes made of sulfur and hydrogen.

lahar- A flow of water mixed with ash

and rocks, which can be like a swift river of concrete. Lahars can be very destructive, destroying buildings and carrying huge boulders. A volcano does not need to be erupting for a lahar to occur. "Lahar" is the Indonesian word for "mudflow."

lava- Molten rock when it is above ground.

lava dome- Mounds of lava made from lava too sticky (viscous) to flow down the volcano in a lava flow. Volcanoes that build up in lava domes are usually much more explosive than volcanoes with runny lava, like Hawaiian volcanoes.

magma- Molten rock when it is underground.

monitoring- Watching and measuring the conditions at a volcano to see what it's doing.

pyroclastic flow- A hot, quickly-moving flow of gas, ash, and rocks of different sizes. Pyroclastic flows often move faster than a car and can be MUCH hotter than an oven.

seismometer- An instrument that measures any shaking in the ground. These days, most seismometers are digital and are able to radio-transmit their data to scientists who can instantly look at and analyze the measurements. Seismometers

used at volcanoes are so sensitive they can even measure strong winds, ocean waves hitting the shore, shaking when a helicopter lands on the ground, or critters stomping around.

sulfur dioxide- (SO_2) A gas released by volcanoes made of sulfur and oxygen.

swarm- A series of earthquakes happening over a short period of time.

thermal camera- A special kind of camera that can measure the temperature of the surface of an object. A thermal camera detects light that our eyes can't see (infrared light) to determine temperature.

tsunami- A very dangerous series of waves made when water is quickly shoved out of place. They can be created in different ways, such as when an earthquake, a pyroclastic flow, or a landslide quickly shoves seawater out of place.

vent- The location where gas or lava comes out of a volcano.

volcanologist- A scientist that studies volcanoes.

volcano-tectonic earthquake- A type of earthquake made when gas or magma breaks rock inside a volcano as it moves.

About the Author

Sonja loves volcanoes! She earned her Masters degree in geology and since then, she's worked at volcanoes in Montserrat (West Indies, Caribbean), Craters of the Moon in Idaho (USA), and Mount St. Helens in Washington (USA). Her work has also taken her to volcanoes in Italy, Mexico, and the Canary Islands. In her spare time, she's out exploring with her kayak, rockhounding, doodling, sticking her nose in a good book, or playing with her dog Pepper. This is her first book.

Acknowledgements

Sonja warmly thanks those that encouraged and helped her in the process of creating this book. Thanks first and foremost to Brandon Chiasera and Melanie Froude, who gave invaluable support throughout the entire process of making this book and who provided a plethora of helpful comments and edits. Thanks to Dr. Erouscilla Joseph, Stacey Edwards, and Dr. Joan Latchman at the University of West Indies Seismic Research Centre (UWI-SRC) for helpful edits. Thanks also to Montserrat Volcano Observatory and UWI-SRC for institutional support. Finally, Sonja thanks her numerous colleagues and friends whose kind words gave her the confidence to go for it and make this book!

Made in the USA
Monee, IL
11 February 2020